Stay Safe

And Kiss the Babies

*Delightful COVID-19 reflections from 100
days on a Great-grandmother's back porch*

Bonnie Huber

*Dedicated to my best friend and husband
of 60 years, Ken Huber.*

*And to all of the front line workers
who risk their lives every day to save ours*

Day 1

LOCKDOWN

March 18, 2020, Day 1. Lockdown for NYS I guess this virus is really real. We are all in quarantine NY. At first I thought those girls of mine were just telling me I had to stay in, not go to work because they want me home. Kathy, Kim, Karen and Kendra all said the NO word to me. (I abhor the no word) But Gov. Cuomo said the no word! It's a lockdown. So people, we need to protect our loved ones. Stay in, Stay safe and Kiss the babies.

Day 2

THE LINEN CLOSET

March 19, 2020, Day two of house arrest. Cleaned out my linen closet. Had things in there from my bridal shower 1960. So on to my closets tomorrow. Marcy coming to visit. But bringing wine to kill any germs we may have.

Day 3

CLOSET DRINKING

March 20, 2020, Day Three of lock down. If I'm cleaning closets today and Marcy brings wine, is that considered closet drinking? Just asking for a friend.

Day 4

NOT A PAINTER

March 21, 2020, Day 4. Decided to paint the little foyer. Gray/Blue. White woodwork. But. Got gray on the white. White on the gray. Gray on the white. Again. You get it.

Day 5

CRUEL CHILDREN

March 22, 2020, Day five. Well I'm in solitaire today. Evidently I have attitude!!!!!! I'm thinking it's Elder abuse. And No one is asking my side of the story.

Day 7

REFLECTIONS

March 24, 2020, Day 7. Reflections. Sitting here watching the birds. Listening to my James Taylor music, thank you Kim. Thinking how very rich I am. Rich and blessed. I have to stay in my warm house that my dear Ken built for us. Look at all I have and all he left me. My dear siblings and their mates. My four beautiful, caring, loving daughters. Add in the sons they married. The wonderful thoughtful grandchildren and their mates. Add in my bonus. The 6 great grandchildren. They gave me life again after Ken. The baseball, the soccer, the basketball, the dancing and gymnastics. The caring and respect they all show me. The babies. (Who are adorable) the pride I have for what Ken left me. The dear friends old an new. From high school to Kens brother's family and friends and their wives. To our sport families who are also my family. I just want you all to know you are all loved and God bless you all as I am Blessed . Thank you to all my loves

Day 8

SO BORED

March 25, 2020, Day 8 Lockdown. Found the book I bought last year on procrastination. Going to read it today. Or maybe tomorrow.

Day 9

THE NEW NORMAL?

March 28, 2020, Day 9. Trying So hard to keep it positive. Watching less news. Staying in. Walking Gilligan Road. Just missing what we have all been taking so for granted. Pretty much everything normal. Especially miss my family and friends. Let's pray it's over soon.

Day 10

BIRD WATCHING

March 29, 2020, Day 10. Watching the dog watching the birds. I'm ok today. It's Sunday and I have hope. I dug down deep and found Betty Tillson's (MY MOM) Get up you'll feel better, so I'm up again Just have to share. In times of crisis people want to know that you care. They don't care what you know. Stay Safe. Stay in. Throw the cook a kiss.

Day 12

LOVE

March 31, 2020, Day 12. I missed a day. We were playing Wine Scrabble. It's a lot like Scrabble. But with Wine. Reflecting today. I believe this is ail happening to slow down the world. We are all going 50-to 100 miles an hour. Both parents and single moms and dads are working two jobs or long hours. No time to spend with kids or their parents. On our Sunday ride we saw some dads out in the yard playing with their kids. We are all being forced to stay home, to be together. We see our essential workers taking such a risk. Nurses Doctors Nurses Aides. All service workers are our heroes now. We are all seeing what is important. It's our loved ones. Realizing it's just our loved ones. This virus is beyond horrible. I believe everything happens for a reason. Love your loved ones. Keep your babies safe. Be safe. Stay in. You are loved.

Day 13

ANNE FRANK

April 1, 2020, Day 13. April fools does not seem appropriate. Had some things of encouragement this AM. But cannot get Roger's post out of my mind. Anne Frank. She hid in an attic room for 25 months. Was discovered, captured, taken to a concentration camp in November 1944. Died March 1945 at 15 years of age. So I know we all have it difficult at this time. But not Anne Frank difficult. Count our blessings. Thanks Roger for making me see some light in our dilemma. Throw kisses, love your people. Call your person. Keep your chin up.

Day 14

NOT EVERYONE CAN FORAGE FOR THEMSELVES

April 2, 2020, Day 14. Reflecting this morning. Watching the birds. Last day of feed. It's time for them to forage on their own. I think of it as a type of welfare. Get them through bad times (winter) and then they are on there own. But birds differ from people. Not everyone can forage for themselves. So we do not judge. Please do not judge. I've been reading FB anger, complaining, criticism, worry. Let's try to be an encourager in this time of critics, pick up others that are down. Count your Blessings. Stay in. 6 feet away. Tell your people you love them. Be ever so careful out there. Keep your babies safe. Blow the cook a kiss.

$\mathcal{D}ay$ 15

ELDER ABUSE

April 3, 2020, Day 15 Lockdown (with attitude) so I've Been informed. Daughter Kim is going to the grocery and wine store. I've also been informed I am not going. I tried to override with her sisters. but they are all saying No to me. (hate the word) There is just tooo many of them and I'm an old frail lady. It's just total disrespect for ones dear Mother. So. I'm going to report them all for elder abuse The Dr always asks how are things at home, anyone abusing you, and I'm going to say yes now and tell the whole sordid story. If you happen to ride by my house just know it's a house of horrors in there. So Kim will pull out of the driveway leaving me here without any remorse. I just hope I get to post tomorrow. If you don't see my post call my sister Denise. If you call those girls they will just laugh and say she's fine. But you all know the real story. Be safe, stay in, love your people. Keep those baby's safe. Blow the cook a big kiss.

Day 16

A BROKEN HEART

April 4, 2020, Day 16. Sorry my Facebook Friends. No post today. My heart is broken I had to put down my Mollie Dollie this morning. 17 years we had her. Maybe tomorrow.

Day 21

CAROL BURNETT

April 9, 2020, Day 21. Lockdown. Humiliation with humor yesterday I was on the phone when my daughter asked me what I had going on here. I said what??? Sooo, I had on a plaid nightgown. To my calf. Gray heavy knee socks, turquoise sneakers (I had gone out to get the paper.). A gray housecoat also with stars, to the calf. And my baseball hat. She said I looked like Carol Burnett with out the pail and mop. Kim said I needed to step up my game. I guess being locked in the house and looking at that getup is not her idea of nice. Sooo , today I got dressed. Be safe out there my friends stay in (maybe get dressed.)

Day 22

DONE WITH THIS ISOLATION

April 10, 2020, Day 22. Lockdown . Soon I'll be sitting out on the deck. That will be grand. The only thing wrong is not seeing the girls and children. This whole stay home thing makes us realize even more (if we did not already) just what is important. Our loved ones. It also slowed down the rat race for many. Many are still out there working and taking chances, did not get the rest and pause we all got. Many are just making it or maybe not making it, with no pay. I pray for you. Hopefully this will be over soon and we can go back to our loved ones. That's about all we can go back to. Life has changed. But our people are here for us. I can't wait to see them hug them kiss their cheeks. And hear the question, table of booth. ?? To be with dear friends. Stay in, Be safe, Be thankful, Pray for those less fortunate and all the people on the front lines.

Day 22

GARTH BROOKS

April 11, 2020, Day 22. Lockdown. Just heard the song If tomorrow never comes will they know how much I loved them. Garth Brooks. Will they?? Having lost so many loved ones already. I don't believe I expressed how much they all meant to me. Why are we somewhat reserved when expressing love? My Ken never knew that I thought he could walk on water. Too late now. My best friends Butchie and Bonnie did not know how I truly felt about them and revered them. Too late. My Mother. How much I admired her for so many reasons. I guess what I am saying is please let your loved ones know just how much they mean to you before it's to late and you all have is regrets. Now is the time when we all realize just how much we love. Be safe. Stay in you are loved.

Day 24

WORDS WITH FRIENDS

April 13, 2020, Day 24. Sitting. Looking out the window. Thinking about the situation. 4 weeks we've been in lockdown. I'm ok. I'm old, it is what it is. But I have a bad habit (well probably a lot of them). When I have something on or in my mind and I just blurt out what I'm in the middle of thinking. So, family, try To figure what the he— I'm talking about. It's like a guessing game with no damn clues. Me: Guess where SHE went last week. Daughters,: Mom I don't know who she is and don't know where she went!!! Me: do you know what time he gets up in the morning. Again. They have to come back with. Nope. Don't know who he is and certainly don't know what time he gets up. And I think they don't care either. So I'll continue this game. I love it. Drives them crazy. Just like they used to do to me. A lot of fun. Try it.. Kim says it's like cooking for the home . Stay safe my friends. Distance 6 ft. Stay in.

Day 25

CONTEMPLATING THE CURRENT REALITY

April 14, 2020, Day 25. Lockdown So much time now to put things in the right boxes in our homes, and also in our heads. A little organizing. Perspective. We can now realize what Is important. Family. And our Friends. It's not just eating out, meeting for a drink, or dinner or lunch, it's who we're meeting, it's our loved ones! Its the old and new close and not so close friends we are so glad to see, give a smile, shake hands and a Hug. Its the Hi glad to see you. You look great. It's the ones we are missing. Who we are without. It does not mean we're lonely. It means we truly need our friends. And especially our family we are separated from. I always believe everything happens for a reason. And this happened to help us stop and slow it down and smell the flowers. I don't feel we will take anyone for granted going forward. I can't wait to be with all my people. My friends, My loves My reason for being. Be careful, stay home, be safe.Stay 6 feet. Kiss the babies.

Day 26

AMAZON:
MY NEW BEST FRIENDS

April 15, 2020, Day 26. Lockdown Getting ready to take a shower I feel if we smell good it may help us feel good. My friend needs hair color so I ordered it from Amazon. Gonna step up my game. I think my friend is going to need larger size clothes for our coming out party. Won't that be Grand. Have not used makeup for duration. So saving $$$. I'm looking at all the leaves I blew off Sunday and annoyed my neighbors. They all blew back yesterday. So maybe I'll get to that point tomorrow. I don't want to rush into anything and besides I'm real busy!! We are saving so much $$ staying in we're making it up on Amazon. Cushions, a new snake hose, a gas heater for the deck, gift for baby, biggy. Jeans. They come about every day and leave it on the deck. It's like presents all week. I believe we're totally in the red about now. I can't wait to be standing in the driveway, flowerbed work, raking and just outside. We're going to make it through, I feel it. Be safe, Stay in, you are loved. Soon.

Day 28

SO?   I FORGOT!!

April 17, 2020, Day 28.   Lockdown Well I'm in trouble again. I'm not allowed to talk to Kim all day. Let me tell you my side of the story and remind all I'm "79.". I had a Visa card from Verizon , $55.00. A refund from turning off my house phone in January. It's going to expire the end of this month. I hate to lose $$ so I kept on Kim (nagging) to take it when she went grocery shopping. Well she did. And when she came home she informed me there was a pin and she could not use it. Well I do remember using it once and no pin. Soooo I called Verzion ready for battle. And he very nicely said Just use it as a credit instead of debit. So I'm good with that and then he felt the need to tell me that's not why my card was declined. It's because it only has $2.36 left on the card. It had been used at CVS., Tractor store and

TJ Mack's. I was really Oh, right, now I remember all that. Sooo Kim will only take cash going forward. And I can't look at her today. So much like her father. She is so on top of everything. Again I'm 79. There is so much in my head !!

Day 29

NOT DRESSED FOR BATTLE

April 18, 2020, Day 29. Lockdown. Not much going on today. Kim made Blueberry pancakes for breakfast. Ravioli with spinach-for lunch. Chip and dip for a snack.. Wine time, now, waiting for dinner. Played trivia with Kristin and Kendra. So I'm gonna tell you about something that happened (always about me) lol. In July I went to Kristins apartment to help her move out and clean the apartment. I was gonna work so I had cut off khakis, no socks and acqua sneakers. And a Minnie Mouse tee shirt. I helped in the heat for a few hours with no AC. So when I left and was on my way home I realized I needed 1/2 and 1/2. I kinda knew what I looked like. but did not want to go all the way home. change and come back. I thought I could just sneak in Aldi's; in and out. Went quickly down the aisle to milk area. Got in and around the aisle, on way to check out. But noo, someone was actually following me and said Hi, do you remember me? i said oh sure. (I did not.). She said oh I remember you. I used to be so jealous of you when we were young. Sooo , I got a little puffed up, feeling ok about myself AND then she said, Yes , I always wondered how you ever got Kenny. Who the hell ever says that. And to someones face. I could not even reply when I realized what the hell I had on. I said. well nice seeing you whoever you are. I went home And called Kristin to tell her about it and she could not stop laughing. She said Grandma I can't believe you went in the store. I looked in the mirror. And I can't believe I did either. My story. Wanted to give you all a laugh. Be safe, stay in, Kiss the babies.

Day 30

SO? I'M 79!!

April 19, 2020, Day 30. Lockdown. Sunshine. Going to blow leaves off the deck and sit out this afternoon. It's like going out. Denise wants me to tell you this story. Once upon a time a young girl (me) was dating a boy from Chatham. His mother, we'll call her Creulla, did not like me a little bit. He had dated a nice girl from a really good family from Chatham before I came on the scene. Creulla called me MaryAnn for the first 10 times I went there. Fast forward about 10 years. Everybody married to others, everybody very happy. I got a call from a neighbor whose daughter needed to go to the dentist. Lot of pain. No car. So I hurried to get ready. We were having company for dinner so I was dressed with makeup. I have two pair of stretch pull on boots, brown and black. When I was in the dentist waiting room. I saw Creulla's sister come in. I immediately felt uncomfortable and unsure. She said. Oh hello. How are you, Are you still married. I sat there and got my self all back together. All pumped up. Ready to take her on. And made eye contact. And thought I have makeup on, I have my hair done and I'm dressed for the damn occasion. And I have, Omg, I have my boot on the wrong foot its facing in. Sooo , I slowly put the crossed leg boot down by the other boot (hoping she did not notice). Got them put together, And one was black the other was brown. So I Slid them slowly way under my chair. To this day I don't know if she noticed the boots or the fact that I limped out. She probably told them I have something wrong with my feet. Be safe stay in wash your hands and kiss the baby.

Day 31

SNEAKING OUT OF THE STORE

April 20, 2020, Day 31. Lockdown   Got dressed yesterday. Taa daa. Kendra and Denise stopped by. We did the 6 feet thing. Ordered pizza from Piez . They deliver. It was soooo good. Now for the rest of the story. Way back, sometime in the girls young years, I went shopping for Thanksgiving. (biggie shopping). Really crowded. As I'm in my own world concentrating and all that, over the loud speaker came the announcement: Would everyone check their carts; someone has the wrong cart,! Of course you know who. The woman right near me said Can you imagine all those groceries and having to start over. I agreed with her wholeheartedly. Sooo I slowly walked to the meat section at the back of store. Walked along the meats. Away from the cart. Toward the dairy aisle. Left at dairy. Slowly, don't draw attention. Walking a little faster. Left at next aisle, do not run. Right, Left, smile. Get that panic look off your face. Yeah, found my abandoned cart Finished Shopping. Got to my car. No one knew. I was safe. When I got in the car. I laughed and I laughed all the way home. When I pulled the car in garage. I was still laughing. I heard Ken say to the girls. Oh no what did she do now. Why would he say such a thing. Be safe. Stay in. Kiss the babies.

Day 32

MY MOTHER-IN-LAW
ON MY HONEYMOON??

April 21, 2020, Day 32. Well, its day 32 lockdown for me. 3 days in solitary (not to bad) 2 days not allowed to talk. (not bad). I think I'm battin a thousand. Now for the rest of the story. Way back in the Olden days, 1960. I got married to my guy. We went to NYC on our Honeymoon. Now I was 19. Had lived in Greenport and Stottville. The end. Never went anywhere. At all. So, we are at the hotel and Ken parks and goes inside to check in. Some strange man came up to our car and motions for me to roll down the window. I did, but @2 Inches. He said I'm here to take your luggage. Well I was suspicious. So I said no I'm waiting for my husband (that sounded so good, my husband). The man said he told me to come get your luggage. I again said I'm waiting. So he went back inside and came back with Ken. Who said. Bon unlock the doors and get out of the car. Sooo we go inside the man following us. In front of me are moving stairs. (later known as an escalator.). I said how do we get on this.? Ken must have seen the fear in my eyes and said, We'll take the elevator. Fast forward. The next day Ken took his pants to the tailor to be hemmed. There was also a shoeshine right in the building. So he said I'm gonna get a shoe shine. Wait for the pants. Sooo I'm sitting looking at a magazine. When what the he—!! They page my mother-in-law over a mike that the pants are ready. I'm like wth. Why is his mother here ? I'm seriously looking all over for her. So I cant locate her. And they paged again, now I'm really annoyed. And a young boy comes up to me and said your husband said to go get the pants. I looked over at him. and he had the first I can't believe you look I ever saw from him. Many more to come over in the 50 years! But you just have to admit it, was never boring And his mother was not really there. I was

Mrs. Huber. Be safe. Stay in. Remember 6 feet. Soon it will be better. Kiss the babies.

Day 33

THE SNAKE

April 22, 2020, Day 33. Lockdown, Busy day. Our Icemaker is down. I found and filled and made own Ice. Pretty good huh. Kim and I were sitting at the kitchen table and she said Mom is that a stick or a snake on the deck. Well it was a snake. It was moving so slowly across the deck. We googled it and it looked so much like a copper head. The young neighbor Keith was mowing and I asked him if he could help. He said it's a Milk Snake. He was so nice and tried to pull it out from under our porch. But it was coiled and would not budge so he had to let him go. So that being said., Kim and I are moving. We will send you our forwarding address as soon as we find it. Be safe, stay home (yet) and I can see the horizon of this coming soon. Kiss the babies.

Day 36

FOND MEMORIES

April 25, 2020, Day 36. Hunkering down I went into work Friday. Just two of us in the office. And one from another property helping out. Did not let anyone else in. Got new masks from boss in mail. (Thank you Conifer!) Now going way back to 1945 and the end of World War II and Maple Ave. This was before McDonalds, Burger King and Dunkin Donuts. There was a beautiful dairy farm near by, Healys Farm. (My brothers worked there delivering milk before school.) Maple Avenue. We knew every neighbor on the street. We could walk to the end and there was Greenport school. We could play in the street as no one had cars. And no TVs. My best friends Butchie, Janice, Elaine and Elizabeth. We were out all day as the houses were so small we would have driven our parents crazy (never allowed). We had an ice man that would come in a truck with ice covered with canvas. If you needed ice you put a card in your window and he would cut it and bring it right in your house. To your ice box. No refrigerators here. A coal furnace that my brothers had to feed when home from school and mom working. They would deliver coal and shoot it right into your cellar window. We had no hot water. Had to heat water for baths. There was a little Mom and Pop store at head of street and around the corner. Mom had a charge account there for us. We would charge cheese, bread , chef boyardi spaghetti and lemon meringue pie. Jack was in charge. He would cook for us as we were not to touch the stove. (coal). He took such good care of me. There was rationing of meat, bacon, butter sugar, cheese, eggs and cooking fat. Milk too, but we got that from the farm. This was right up til the 50's. There was a coupon system. And you had to be registered at a particular store. Moms choice was Sams Super Market as his meat was so good. Now I'm going to mention Edna Mae Johns our baby sitter. The best dear sweet person I know. She was my salvation. So kind to us. And I love her dearly. I am so happy and grateful for the wonderful childhood I had. And my point after all that reminiscing is this: We lived through world War 2, Korea, Vietnam, Gulf War, and Iraq and Iran. And this pandemic tops all,. Never could have seen this coming. But we will survive. We're tough. God bless America. Be safe, stay in. Wear your mask. 6 ft apart . Kiss the babies.

Day 37

THE SIMPLE TASK

April 26, 2020, Day 37. Lockdown. Put our heater/stove for the deck together yesterday. I was not happy as it came from China. Trying only to buy American! It's nice I have to admit. Now for the rest of the Story. Way back in early 80's. Home alone. I was in the house cleaning. And thought (that was when this trouble started). It's a beautiful day I think I'll burn the garbage. So I took the trash out and started burning! I came in and continued cleaning. A little while later I saw my window all fogged. clouded over. It was smoke. I ran outside and the leaves around the burn barrel were on fire. I ran to the hose. The car was parked on the hose. The Ran to house for car keys and moved the car. More leaves , more smoke. Turned on water. The water was turned off from the house. I found that faucet and turned on the water, ran toward the fire, but the hose was too short. More leaves, more smoke. SO I had to call Fire Dept. The Fire was moving up the hill about 50 to 1OO feet wide. I would have burned down West Ghent....The West Ghent Fire Dept was there in a flash (seemed like an hour to me) I was a wreck. They had it out in 10 minutes. (leaves sure make a lot of smoke.). Richard and Jonathan Kozel were on the fire truck and they calmed me back down. And then could not stop laughing. Thank you again Richard and Jonathan. You saved my life. Needless to say I never burned the garbage again to this day. Still not one of my best memories. Stay safe, stay in. Wear your mask. We are on our way out of this. Kiss the babies.

Day 38

A LEOPARD GIRDLE

April 27, 2020, Day 38. Lockdown. Better attitude, feeling the light is at the end of the tunnel!!! I stepped up my game. My sweat pants matched my sweater. Blended grays. I'm trying. Being home and every time I open the refrigerator slowly, quietly there is no little fluffy dog Molly looking up, What you got Mon??? You eating??? I'm hungry too or if I'm having dinner, Oh that looks good!! Watching every bite. So I'm totally dining alone and it's really strange. My story today is. The leopard Girdle. Once upon a time, 1961. I was in the hospital having my daughter Kathleen. Baby born, very beautiful, it was all over and I was at a sink in my room washing my hands. I have to share : I'm very modest (we were kinda weird in the 50's so my daughters tell me). I saw the Dr coming and ran as fast as I actually could so he did not see me in my Pajamas. Now mind you this man had just delivered my baby. Silly me. The Dr told me to find the tightest girdle I could, put it on and keep it on. So I told my Mom. Who else ??? I had never owned a girdle. Weighed in about 100. My mother brings me a leopard satin girdle with black lace on bottom and black stocking hooks There was a nurse in the room when I opened it and she could not stop laughing. I was mortified. The nurse told everyone on the ward and they all took turns asking to see it. In the 60's no one wore leopard. And sure as hell the Dr came in and said OK let's see that leopard girdle everyone is talking about. My face was so red I could feel the fever. He laughed really hard and then says to me (who had nothing at all to do with this) Now don't come back pregnant for your 6 week checkup. OMG. Like I was a real swinger. Thanks Betty Tillson!! She sure gave the whole Maternity Ward a good laugh. As for me, you can see I never forgot it. Love You Mom Love your sense of humor. You were always trying to lighten me up. Stay safe....6 feet, wear the mask and kiss the babies.

Day 39

BEWARE OF YOUR CHILDREN

April 28, 2020, Day 39. Makeup jeans, Big day out. Hannaford. I had my mask. They have one way aisles. Everybody doing the 6 ft. Just a few coming down the enter aisle backwards. You cannot help these people.. I went to the bottle return to get more scan tags for my bottles and there was a cart full of black bags of bottles parked in the way. A worker in a big plastic shield asked if they were mine I said no. He said what am I supposed to do with them ??? I didn't know how to answer as I don't work there! We were leaving the area with him pushing the cart full of bags and me walking along side him. A women came charging at us and said is that my cart of bags? What are you doing with them? Was someone trying to steal them ??? He said why did you leave them there? She said why do you have them. I said he works here. He's just doing his job. She'd said who the hell are you? I said good bye and went in the store. Sooo, almost had a good outing. Then on to liquor store. No issue there .. Now I'm going to let you all know I have been talking to Ken Huber's daughters; they all visited today. And they spent the afternoon Rolling their eyes - behind my back, snickering at me. Talking like I was not in the room. When I went to the bathroom I tried to hear what they were saying but I did not hear the word " the home or she's senile". So I felt it's ok. So far. My side of the story. In my defense I say, I'm going down cellar. When no one cares. I say I'm gonna check the mail and no one asked. I ask has anyone seen my Phone, glasses, Drink, keys. A lot I say "what did you say" all day long. I ask Oh, are you doing laundry when they go by with a basket full of clothes. But I love when they tease me and laugh at my silly. I love their joking about me with each other. Their father showed his affection that way. And they learned from the best. We do say I love you. And hug. But they really show it by roasting

Mom. But. I still have to be on my toes because there are 4 of them. I make believe I don't hear them and listen into their conversations. I can even hear when they whisper but they don't know. I've made it through another winter. Remember how the Indians would take the old people out in the woods and leave them there in the wintery snowy nights. Well I'm not gonna fall for that. I got this. Winter is over.!! Stay Safe and kiss your babies.

Day 41

MODESTY AT CAMP

April 30, 2020, Day 41. Lockdown. Rainy day so it's ok to be lazy and not mind too much staying in. Watching ELLEN on tv. Rusting. My mom always said. You rest you rust. Well I'm sure rusting and eating and drinking and eating. My diet started this morning. I had cottage cheese, banana and strawberries. Good. Then I had a Piece of oat toast. So I'm already over my carb count for the day. So I'll have to start the diet tomorrow. So then I had a BLT. It's all good. I'll start for sure tomorrow. I'm officially over my pregnant weight. Attractive. And now for the rest of the story. We have so much time on our hands and my age I go back way back in times that jump out of the vault. My mom was a single mom. My brothers both went to Boys Club camp at Camp Anderson in Kinderhook for two weeks. My Maple Ave friend Elaine Marshall won a

Girl Scout trip to the Adirondack's. I wanted to go to so I asked my mom. The cost was $40.00 a week. Mom barely made that total but she found a way. She always did. So we got to the Adirondack's, camp Hidden Lake. We were put in lean-to's and one whole side had no wall. Scary. There were 4 bunks. One Albany girl cried for half the night. The next day we had a fun busy day and swimming in afternoon. We were told to bring 2 bathing suits. If one was wet let it dry. I left it on the bunk and when I came back there were porcupine quills all over the suit. Our Albany girl started to cry. Again. None of us slept too well that night. The next day was pretty much more of the same. BUT, the next morning we were awakened, and told to take off our PJ's and grab just our towels. (both of our suits were damp) . So with nothing on but a towel we followed the counselors to the lake. Then we were told to drop our towels and go into the lake. Well I don't know which was worse. The water was @ 35 degrees or if I'm naked. I was so modest. I was 10. So I almost hyperventilated. Albany is crying. One counselor said they wanted us to get over our modesty !! The days all ran into each other. During the nights, I think we all joined Albany crying. knowing we get to do this all again in the AM

So if you were not able to go to Girl Scout Camp, see what you missed. My mom said she wished she had kept my post cards. I asked her to come to get me every day,   This is just a chapter in why I'm so weird. What does not kill you makes you stronger. (or a little weird) be safe. Still stay 6ft. And kiss the babies.

Day 43

DRUNK DRIVING

May 2, 2020, Day 43. Lockdown. I went out yesterday. To work. Did not let anyone in the office. Had my mask ready. Felt good to work. My story today. I'm sitting here looking out at a beautiful day. Thinking how I'm going to visit a friend this afternoon and have a glass of wine. (1) I'm driving. This reminded me of once way back about 4 years ago. I went to a friend's barbecue. 4th of July. I was there @ 2:00—8:00. I had 2 glasses of wine over 6 hours, as I never never drink and drive. As I was near leaving my friend said "here try this wine my nephew brought from Texas". I tried it but did, not drink a glass. I left. Came out of Mellenville Road onto route 217. Double lines. Sped up to @ 50. Took A right on Gahbauer Rd. A Trooper came up behind me with lights on so I pulled over in the grass. He said he pulled me over because I was doing 55 in a 30. I never saw a sign!!! He said have you been drinking tonight. I said yes I had two wines. He said you need. to get out of the car. He was my height (@5'5. He used the follow the light test first. Walk a straight line. Now mind you I was in heels and on a bank on a back road. He said your a little wobbly. Really???? Then he said I'm gonna have to give you a breathalyzer . Well I was not even breathing at this time. All I could think of was calling my daughters. I never ever would heard the end of that. All my many boring lectures about drinking and driving. My name in the police blotter in the paper. I knew I only had 2 wines all day. But I did not know how that damn thing was gonna come out, i was about ready to go out! Well I passed the test. But got a big lecture about if I had had an accident that evening it would be my fault because I was drinking. So to this day. I will only have (1) wine. I was 75 at the time. And he was soooo rude. He treated me like I could not walk and just robbed a gas station and hid the gunshot. I think he wanted me to fail. But Taa daa!! A valuable lesson for this ole gal! Be safe. If you go out. Keep your 6ft. Kiss the babies.

Day 44

CRUELLA

May 3, 2020, Day 44. Lockdown. My daughters are together today. Doing the 6ft. They needed time out from their mother. Can you imagine that??? I don't get it. So I'm going way back to 1950. My brothers got to go to Boys Club Camp Anderson in Valatie for 2 weeks. And i got to go to my grandmother Cruella 'Deville's house in Ancram NY. I was 9 yrs old. And think I had ADD but not labeled yet. My Grandma, Cruella, had so many gd rules. If would take a rocket scientist to remember them all. First I think she resented my mom having a break from parenting. Grandma never had a break. But I regress. There was a pump in the kitchen for water and you could pump to wash your hands. But had to wet a wash cloth for your face. Never use the washcloth on your hands. Then you had to hang the washcloth on a rack to use the next time, I could never remember which damn color was mine. Then the best part, under the house in the garage was an outhouse. The rule was if you were up you had to use the outhouse. There were 13 steps from the porch down to the garage. And I had to use a flashlight and walk down the 13 steps, slide open the garage door and go to whatever the hell it was called. You just cannot pull down PJ's, pee and and hold a light all at the same time. I was so afraid a rat would bite me in the buttocks!!! ??? I don't know??? Now if you're in bed. You get to use the pot under the bed. That was supposed to be better. OMG. mom. Come save me. Then in the AM Cruella would ask did you wash your face. I would answer yes. And then wait for it, which washcloth is yours? I don't know. Then did you use the washcloth on your hands? I don't know. Then, Wait for it, did your mother teach you nothing??? Well my mother did not care if I used a washcloth on my face or did not use a washcloth.!! Only water and soap on my hands. My mother did nothing like all this. or have all these rules. My mother was a no rules Mom, It is what it is. So she did not notice my ADD. I learned a lot that summer. That My mom was the best person in the whole world!!

Be safe, 6ft distance. And kiss those babies.

Day 45

SNAKES IN THE CAR

May 4, 2020, Day 45. New spectrum and I'm streaming the HBO Sopranos one of my favorites. I'm into a day and a half.. And daughter called. So i put Sopranos on hold and cannot get back to the episode I was on and it's a really good episode! My remote has a mike on it. And I was asking it to play Sopranos. But I was saying. Lexi, play Sopranos, over and over. Nothing. So my daughter said, Mom, its alexis, not Lexi. And our remote is Siri!! Boy, who knew? Now for the rest of the story. Way back in the olden days @ 1950 ish. My mother would drive us to Ancram every Sunday to see her parents. Cruella and Grandpa Bill, the sweetest man ever. We would be seen but never heard. (unless Grandpa asked us about ourselves.) Well right next to their house is a cemetery. And we were always playing outside. And this day we played in the cemetery. Well my brothers Jackie and Billy (before they were Jack and Bill). came across a nest of baby snakes. Not sure of kind of snake. Well Jack sent Bill to get a can for the babies. And they stuffed them all in a can. And left it outside Grandpas house. Well it came time to motor back to Hudson. Brothers put the Snakes in the trunk of the car and away we went. When we got home. Mom went inside and the boys opened the trunk. There were a few crawling around in the trunk. The rest were all gone. So like boys will be boys, they just went in the house. We never hear Mom scream or mention the snake word. So all was good. I learned so many not-to -do things growing up with those brothers. I learned to keep my mouth shut. Never to squeal. And most of all I learned Love. Thank you brothers.   Be safe. Stay in, masks, 6 ft. And kiss the babies.

Day 46

STRANGER DANGER

May 5, 2020, Day 46. Lockdown. I'm in big trouble (again) I answered a friend on messenger and found out she received a $$ bonus. And she referred me to a WHO site person who asked me for personal information. I thought it was legit because a dear friend told me to do it for a bonus. Butttt it was not my friend. All of a sudden I did not like the English wording and I called my friend. She had no idea what I was talking about. The message even came in with her picture. Then I had to back track and get the he— off that message. Be careful out there. (I got many lectures from the daughters).. Now for the rest of the story. Way back in the 90's. Ken and my son in law were working in Troy. They were having a Holiday party in Troy. So as Ken and my son in law were already there working, my daughter and I drove up together. There was a bad snow storm ans I cold barely see. On 787 there was a loud rumble rumble rumble. I asked my daughter. Is that a train??? She said No Mother it's a flat tire! (they all call me mother when they're exasperated). Sounds so much nicer than No, stupid. Well if you know 787. there is nothing but highway. We were standing out side when a car pulled up and a nice guy asked if we needed help. I asked if he could call Ken at the Eddy and tell him where we were. Nice guy said. I live right near the Eddy. I'll take you there. Soooo we got in the car. Really nice guy. Dropped us off at the Eddy. All Is good. Right??? Told my dear husband the story and where the car was. He handled that and we continued to enjoy the dinner. Soooo we all nicely said our good nights. Went to our different cars. And started home. As soon as the car doors closed. My husband started yelling What the he— is wrong with you getting in a car with a stranger. He could have killed you both. He was not happy I tried to say what a nice guy. Ken said So was Jack the Ripper. The rest of the trip home was so quiet you could hear the snowflakes on the windshield   Not one of my shining moments. Be safe. Wear a mask. 6ft. And kiss the cook and the babies.

Day 48

THE NECK OF A SWAN

May 7, 2020, Day 48. Lockdown. I missed a day. I was so busy but I got a request. This is for Holly and her daughter. Sitting outside this afternoon with feet up not for comfort (in case that damn snake shows up). Went to work today, drove my granddaughter. But I wore my mask. I'm a good girl. And now for the rest of the story. Way back in the good ole late 40's. 47/48 My brother Jackie (aka Jack now) and I went to school at St Mary's Acadamy. We had to walk from Maple Avenue to Glenwood Blvd to get the City bus to 3rd Street. I was 7. So Jack was 10. His job was to watch me. And watch me he did, as our mother had spoken. Well this particular day we were on the return trip. Got to our stop and got off the back door. Jack started for the sidewalk. I had forgotten my little pocketbook sooo I turned around was about to climb the stairs and the bus door closed on my neck. The bus pulled away dragging me along. My legs were running in air. Jack is yelling at the bus driver to stop. Well he did stop, opened the door to see what Jackie was yelling about and I fell out. (problem solved.) People over the years have remarked about my long swan like neck. I never felt the need to explain just why! We did not mention this episode to Betty. Until Jackie was Jack. No sense making a bad situation worse. He really had his work cut out for him being my caretaker. I love this man. Thank you for pretty much everything in my life before Ken and after Ken Be safe stay home if out wear your mask. Wash your hands. Kiss the babies and your significant other.

Day 49

THE HAIRY SWEATER

May 8, 2020, Day 49. Went to work. I was careful. Went to town and. Country. Meatballs Sausage garlic bread. Ready for Sunday. And we will be careful with distance. And now for the rest of the story. If you missed one of my lockdown episode where I was all sweaty, dirty and dressed like a poor homeless person and I needed ½ and ½ for my coffee. Remember when I thought I could slip in Aldis and out and the lady who remembered me and wondered how I ever got Kenny Huber? Well I have given that a real lot of thought and came up with this. I think that Ken thought I was a fast woman, hot tomato, and I'll tell you why and how. We always met at Kelly's. I'd like to say Pub but Kelly's, where the boys were someone waits for me. and it was. Always only Kenny for me ? He had such swagger. But I digress Well this particular night. I wore a drop dead Shagora sweater. It was black like Angora but the hair was longer. It was particularly hot In (the Pub) and I went to the ladies room and discovered the beautiful sweater was shedding all over my body. Long black hair and when I came back and sat down I said to Ken, boy it's hot in here . He said Yes. I then said. This sweater comes off.   Well he sat at attention and said. Are you ready to leave??? I said noooo I mean you autta see me underneath. He said. again Alright Let's go!!! (laughing cause he knew it was going nowhere) . Then I said nooo im all black hair under here. So then he said Oh well let's just forget it. So that's the story of how I got Kenny Huber. The hairy sweater story. He figured anyone that naive will be easy to be with. If nothing else lots of laughs. And laugh we did. So now she has her answer. Be Safe. Wear your mask. Do the 6ft. Kiss the babies.

Day 50

DRIZELLA

May 9, 2020, Day 50. Can you actually believe this ? Not sitting on the porch. All that Snow. But it is way to cold. Hit Town and Country yesterday. Such good food. I may get dressed today.. And now for the rest of the story. Got this out of the vault for Annie Gyr Seltzer. And of course Barb and Judy. Way back in the good ole days, 1957. Arlene . (Beanie) was the prettiest girl in Stottville. But also the prettiest in Hudson High. She was older than me and the fact she let me hang around with her amazed me. I would sit and watch her put her makeup on, which she did not need. In awe, that's probably why she let me in. Who does not like worship? Well this particular night. we had a ride/friend. That's a nice guy that will ride you anywhere just to be seen with you. Well we wanted to go to the Spencertown grange dance - 15 miles.

Too far to walk. I'll never forget how pretty she looked. I always felt like Cinderella's step sister Drizella. But I regress. Ride/friend. got tired of us ignoring him at the dance, peeled out left us there. I don't know who would have been worse Betty or Pearl if we did not get home. Arlene Walked up to a nice looking guy and said. Do you know anyone going to Hudson. He said well I am. He was not, but thrilled to be the chosen one. He held the door open for Arlene. And looked at Drizella like, oh crap you're coming too (can't you walk.) You get in the back seat. So good for self esteem Well you probably know, we made it home. Soon after that Arlene started dating Hank, her husband. I believe he was totally in awe of her also. Gone way to soon dear Beanie.. Stay safe wear your mask. 6ft. Kiss the cook and the babies.

Day 52

LOVING DAUGHTERS

May 11, 2020, Day 52. Great day yesterday. Daughters, son-in-law Rick. (who worked in my yard). Nephew, Granddaughters, granddaughter in law. Great granddaughters And great grand dogs. All tried to do the safe distancing. And now for the rest of the story. My girls told me they were really there for an intervention. Told me I have to step up my game, but slow my role???? Tune in, pay attention. Stop climbing up on chairs to clean the glass on lights. Stop running up and down stairs. They want my washer up stairs. Basically I can't have any darn fun at all. They think I'm old. They make me laugh so hard, because they think I'm actually going to pay attention. Payback Is priceless. I look at them square in each of their eyes and say. I know. I won't do that or I will do that whichever fits the story. It's hard to answer correctly cause I'm only half listening. They are such good daughters. They make me laugh. Talking about my singing and whistling to the oldies. My looking for my cell, my glasses, my wallet etc... (I'm not allowed to ask until I've looked on my own for 10 minutes.) They laugh at my asking stupid questions. They can actually talk about me while I'm in the room. They just have to lower their voices a little, We have fun and laughs and love. The only thing we don't have is the Dad.. Be safe. Stay in a little longer. Distance. And kiss your babies. And if your fortunate to have a significant other kiss them.

Day 55

LIFE IN THE 50's

May 14, 2020, Day 55. Oh My, so hard to believe. Working this AM. Being safe. Wore my mask. Let No one in office. Beautiful ride to Coxsackie. Weather gives us a good outlook. And now for the rest of the story, having grown up in the 50's which were such happy innocent times. I can't help but compare the distance we have come away from the simple freedom we experienced then. My mother had an aunt and uncle who lived in Brooklyn NY in a (to me huge) Brownstone. They wanted me to come visit them. So my mom, who never ever did not give us an opportunity to venture forth, said sure. Mom pushed us out of the nest and I am forever grateful for that. Well mom thought it would be a great experience and her Uncle sent money for a train ticket I was nine years old. Here I was at the Hudson train station and on my coat was a note-pinned with my name and my Aunts address. They were to meet me at the information booth in Grand Central. But my mom told me later that the gate was closed off and I was at the wrong Booth. They spread out and found me. Can you imagine. But I did have their address on my coat. I had a wonderful time. And on the return trip I met a man from Scotland who sat across from me. His accent intrigued me. He bought me the biggest Hershey bar I've ever seen. As you know I made it home safe and sound. My mother's mother did not talk to her for 2 weeks for letting me go. Fast forward to 2020 and my mom would have been charged with child neglect. I would have been placed in a foster home. My Scottish friend would have been arrested for being a pedophile. I loved the 50's. Stay safe stay in wear your mask. And kiss your babies.

Day 56

GRADUATES

May 15, 2020, Day 56. I don't know how many days for lockdown. A lot. I have so much time to reflect. And so many memories come back. And now for the rest of the story. So many important meaningful times. Like our 8th grade graduation from Greenport Grammar School. Now this was 66 years ago and I still have memories. So it was very important. That is why I feel sad for them. The excitement of graduation going on to Hudson High. The talk of new white dresses. I totally knew just what I wanted and my Mom and I were going to motor to Albany to get me a dress!! Then the gavel dropped. No money. The other shoe fell and my moms friend at the end of the street called and offered her daughter's dress from 2 years ago. And that as we were both skinny it will fit. Well my mom was so happy. My heart was totally broken.

Times were hard in the 50's So I smiled cause it made my mother smile. My Aunt brought her crinoline in all starched for me to wear. (They were very 'in ' then.) But the dress was not the full one I had dreamed of, so no crinoline. No full dress. The big day came and just to be on the stage with my classmates and given a diploma with my Mom and brother Jack in the Auditorium. I was so happy. And thank you to the lovely Lil Johns at the end of the street for being such a good friend to my mom. You graduate's are in my heart. Be safe, wear your mask, 6ft. Kiss the babies.

Day 58

KEN'S GIFT FROM ABOVE

May 17, 2020, Day 58. Still hunkering down. . Missing my Great grand children. The babies. I do see the grandchildren at 6ft distance. But not the greats. We are all going to appreciate our loved ones so much more than we have in the past.. And now for the rest of the story! My dear little sister-in-law Bettylou, Brother Bill's wife was always the brunt of Ken's teasing. We went on many vacations; Myrtle Beach, Turning Stone Casino, and had many laughs at his picking on her. She loved it as much as we did. At one time he even told her she was going to have to pay him to come to his funeral. And repeated that a few times. Bettylou said how am I gonna pay you. He said "just play my Numbers". Well when Ken passed I could not bring myself to go to Turning Stone with them or Myrtle Beach. When I was finally ready

Bettylou sat in the back with me so I would not feel alone She is so thoughtful. Well we got there , gambled for a few hours and both lost the farm. When we were ready to leave. Bettylou said Oh No we did not play Ken's numbers. So we went to the Roulette Wheel, one of his favorites. Both novices at the game. So we watched for a few minutes and then got $20 worth of chips and placed $5 on his 7/11/32 Well 32 came in right away and paid 240.00. We were ecstatic. I had all our chips in front of me when he spun the wheel again. I had not picked up the $5 on the table. And 32 came in again. Another $240 Well now we're all freaked out. It was overwhelming . The odds of a back to back number coming in are 1,369 to 1. We had told one of the guys at table about it while playing and he said aren't you gonna let it ride. Well hell no we were so ready to cry or throw up, we left. The feeling of Ken being there was strong and we're sure laughing at us. Well she played his numbers as he suggested. AND he came through. There have been other signs and I know there is something and someone waiting for us out there beyond. Looking forward to being with him again.. Be safe. Stay in. Or wear your mask. Kiss the babies.

Day 60

ODDS AGAINST TOMORROW

May 19, 2020, Day 60. Still in lockdown Such a beautiful day. At least we can go outside and enjoy. Starting to open up. Taa daa And now for the rest of the story. Because it's graduation time. And I feel so badly for our graduates. I'm thinking way back to my high school HHS days and many fond memories of 1959. In March of that year a movie was produced in Hudson, Many stars and so much excitement came with it. Harry Bellafonte, Ed Begley!! Odds Against Tomorrow. There was a notice on a bulletin at school and our theater teacher mentioned it in class. Sounded really good to me so I went marching down to a storefront on 7th Street and filled out my information. I must have been pretty bold. For 3 weeks I ran home every day and asked my mom if any calls. And nothing. But one day I came in and she said guess who called. I was so excited!!!! I had to be at the site on a Wednesday ready to work. They gave me a corny line. But because I had a speaking part They paid me $90 a day And double time for Saturday. The average pay at that time was @ $ 40 a week. It was the most exciting thing ever to happen to me ever. The Movie, my graduation and my 18th birthday all in that year. My mom and I did actually motor to Albany and bought a gown for my Senior prom and my dress for graduation. I got to pay for it myself. The prom, The lake, and after party at my house, With Jackie cooking breakfast for 20 kids. The big graduation day and parties were some of my best times ever. I still smile when I remember. Again I repeat myself. My heart goes out to our 2020 graduates. They should not miss out on any of our celebrating them. Maybe if you know or have a friend or family member. Send them a card. Telling them their special. The beginning. Not the end. Be safe. Stay in I, but if you now venture out. Wear your mask still and 6ft. kiss the babies. And your graduates.

Day 62

OOPS!

May 21, 2020, Day 62. Hello out there. I see a light at the end of tunnel. Things opening up slowly but it's a beginning. I'm so happy. Looking forward to being with family and seeing friends. And now for the rest of the story. Have you ever had a really bad date ??? a really bad date? Well I don't know what or why I remember, this way back in high school. There was a boy in school that was so very good looking. He was actually pretty!! Well a friend fixed me up with him on a double date. We got all gussied up. For you youngsters that means took extra care in how we looked. We went to the Spencertown Grange Dance. ? (Exciting huh?). Well I hate to sound mean but beautiful was as dumb as a rock. No, really, he was. It was like being with a third grader. The glow was off, all gone. He was still pretty buttttt, and I know this may sound mean, but I had to fix this nicely. So I asked my friend to help and could we go home now. So I told beautiful a big lie: I did not feel well, have a bad headache and need to go home. On the way home he put his arm around me. I said I'm so sorry (the Headache) so they dropped us off home. We ran In the house, changed out of our gussied dresses, put on Jeans and I drove us to Stans Bar. We walked in joining friends. Were happy to be there. Laughing, smiling. And oh crap guess who's there. Yup beautiful. I felt sick to my stomach. That his feelings would be hurt. He came toward me oh my. Now what. He said Hi, I'm so glad your feeling better. Can I buy you a drink. He was so sweet, he did not know I was a bitch. I sat with him for the rest of the evening. See I'm not totally mean. We never did date again but Remained friends. But yes beauty is In The eye if the beholder. Forgive me for this error of judgment please, it was a learning experience.

Day 65

CROOKS

May 24, 2020, Day 65. Day. Too many. Lockdown. I escaped yesterday. Went to my daughter Karen's. It was so nice to motor to Kinderhook. And now for the rest of the story. We call this one Maple Avenue. In the 40/50's. We lived on This street. We knew every neighbor. Had best friends ever. Jack had Jim. Bill had Donny. I had Butchie. It was so peaceful. My mom worked two jobs then, beautician daytime and waitress on weekends. Daytime, since I was 3, Butchie's mom Nicky babysat me. So we were like sisters. Off hand I can't think of a sweeter lady than Nicky. Mom used to laugh at the radio soap opera's the ladies on the street were addicted to. When she finally stopped work, wherever she was,she had to get home for Days of our Life. At night Edna Mae Johns baby sat us. We all loved her. She was so kind to us. Always let us stay up a little later. When I reached 10 we did not need a sitter anymore. About three times each summer a carnival would, come to the storm track. We had a good friend , Janice , that would go with us. Mom would give me $2.00. But her dad owned a business ,gave her $5 and then she would go in the petty cash box and get a $20. Rides were 25 cents so Janice treated us all night. We were allowed to stay til 9:00 and walk home. We were also allowed to go down street (Hudson). In The summer the 5&10 stores had their doors open and displays outside. This particular day there were pocketbooks out side. So I talked Janice into taking two. On the way home I said you tell your mom my mom bought them and I'll tell my mom your mom bought them. I think I was a criminal mastermind. Sounds good right??? Wrong. When they each thanked each other the jig was up. My mother was always in control and asked where it came from again. I could not lie. She was very quiet. Took me in the car to Woolworth's 5/10 and made me tell the lady what I did. I was mortified! My mom paid her and again was very quiet on the way home. Asked if I learned anything!?? And that was the end of it. I never stole anything again In my life. I did learn something.!!! I feel so blessed to have lived on that street, walked to Greenport school and then Freshman year to HHS. It was a simple, no crime, no stress time. When I look back I realize we were poor. But everyone of our friends and neighbors were poor also. We just never knew. Such Happy days. Thanks for letting me share. The beginning of my no crime ever life. Well we're getting out more now. Be safe be careful. Wear your masks kiss the babies.

Day 67

THE $405 DRESS

May 26, 2020, Day 67. Lockdown. I'm out of time out. Had to make all those children believe I changed my attitude ( ). Yeah I have to be on my toes. And.. Now for the rest of the story. Way back in the day, about 1979. My friend Marcy's husband had a bodyshop. He had an employee that would get clothes out of the Salvation Army bin to use for rags at the body shop. This particular time there was a Black velvet dress that still had the price tag on it $405.00 included with the clothes. Jim gave it to Marcy because it was just such a beautiful dress Then Marcy asked if i could let it out a bit but when I opened the seam you could see where it was matted down. So no is the answer. Sooo Marc said I should try it on. Well let me tell you this dress was made for me so I kept it. Gifted from Marcy. The next Holiday was New Years Eve and we were all going to a big Firehouse gala with a whole table of friends. Ken and I arrived late as he had to pick up cattle at a farm way up north. When we walked in late everybody was there and many exclaimed over my new black velvet dress. Marcy said (really loud) where the hell did you get that dress Salvation Army??? Everybody was what the hell Marcy, what a terrible thing to say. The two of us could not stop laughing and they all wondered why I was not offended.   I wore it again to the Hudson Urban Renewal Award dinner in New Hartford Conn. Fast forward a few years and Ken asked me why I never wore that dress??? I was 10 lbs over the dress limit.!! That dress was once in a lifetime. Thank you Salvation Army˜ and (Marcy for being bustier them me.) The end. Be safe. Still wear your mask. Stay 6ft. And kiss the babies.

Day 68

DO YOU KNOW WHERE KEN IS?

May 27, 2020, Day 68. Beautiful peaceful day. Kendra came out for dinner break. Enjoyed our little get together. Looking forward to History channel. It's "Grant" third night in the series. My guy just loved the civil war history. And now for the rest of the story, Ken had an architect friend at the Eddy, Lenny, and when Ken retired Lenny gave him the most beautiful Mahogany Humidor. Ken was so pleased with the gift. When Ken passed away Jack and Karen went to pick out something to put his ashes in. They came back and said they did not want to spend my money (Actually Kens money.) That there was a Mahogany box for $895. Or a vase that looked like Walmart. for $250. I thought for awhile and went to the living room and brought out Kens humidor. They were ecstatic. They said omg it's just like the one they had for

$895 What is more fitting for my husband to be in!?? He loved his cigars. And then there I was at the viewing and I was standing at the front of the line of all our dear friends. I kept wondering if I could get through this. Taking deep breaths. When I saw Lenny Coming at me. I was so excited to tell him that final resting place was a gift from him. But I guess I was a little too excited and just said. Oh my Lenny do you know where Ken is??!. He actually took a step back thinking I had lost it. If I did not know, who would ? I said No, Kens in the Humidor. He still could not wait to get the hell away from me. Kim was standing next to me. And said. Mom. You just told Lenny Daddy is in the Humidifier. Poor Lenny, he'll never forget that service. We laugh about it now. And family understood I was not really there. The end. Venture out. Be safe. Mask and 6ft. Kiss your loved ones.

Day ??

HOW CAN YOU LOSE A CHILD?

Whatever4 Day...Things are opening up. But we still need to be very careful people. We do not want this monster to rear its ugly head again. And I have more reflections. About 1966. Have you ever misplaced a child? I say misplaced. We were visiting my Navy brother Jack in Newport RI and they lived in a beautiful row of townhouses on the ocean,, each with the similar front and back porches. Jack went off to the hospital to work and Ken went off to walk the grounds of the base. Edie, Jack's wife, and I were with the children. Jim and Kathy, about four years old, went out the front door, followed by Kimmy 3yrs. We were gathering up Karen and Susie's, bags for the trip to the playground and followed them all outside. Kathy and Jimmy came running up to us and I said,

Where is Kim? They did not know. My stomach dropped. I went one way and Edie went the other. Calling her name. Kimmy had a hearing loss at the time and could not hear us calling. There was a man mowing the lawn by a small area near the water and I asked if he had seen a little blond girl. He said no and he had been there the whole morning. Now the panic set in. All I could think of is what I am going to tell Ken. I lost his daughter??? I was sick to my stomach. I ran around the back of the building, calling. No Kim I ran toward the playground, No Kim. This all took about 1/2 hour. I went around the building again, calling and looking, and on someone's porch between two big shrubs, there she sat. I was able to breathe again. Kim said, "I could not find you Mommy". God was with me that day. It was the most horrible terrible feeling ever. To be totally responsible for someone's well being and fall down on the job. Just relating that story to Ken was bad enough yet alone had he witnessed it. When we reflect on our olden days we remember dates that stand out. That was one I would rather put way back and leave there. But it does not work that way. I was so diligent from that day on. Took my job and my position a lot more seriously Again, Thank You God Please stay safe out there. Wear your mask. 6 feet is good. Kiss your babies.

Day 69

TOPLESS BEACH

May 28, 2020, Day 69. Quiet day, peaceful. Because I'm old I love the slow pace we are experiencing. Soon we will be out and about. Saying How you doing friend??? And now for the rest of the Story. My brother Jack reminded me of this debacle. I would rather forget. Way back in the day we would go to visit brother Jack where ever he was stationed in the Navy. This particular time he was a Lieutenant Commander and stationed in Virginia Beach Virginia. Ken and I went to the Officers Club and then the beach with Jack and I was so impressed with how we were treated. (Because we were Jacks guests). I was on my best ladylike behavior. Had to make my brother proud! Well we were on the beach and I went in the Ocean with the kids. I was having a great time in the waves but all of a sudden a wave came in and took me out and back in. At many miles an hour. The grownups were sitting in chairs and on blankets on the beach. And yes, you guessed it, I came in hell bent toward them. That was not bad enough, my bathing suit top was gone. GONE. Someone handed me a towel. But many other officers and families saw my nudity, my top, My brother could not stop laughing, making believe he did not know me and moving down the beach like they were not with me. My poor Ken. The look on his face. His wife was naked. Well we still laugh about my appearance at the Norfolk Navel Officers Club. Jack won't let me put it in the vault The end. Be safe. Go out, wear your mask and do the 6 feet. Kiss the babies.

Day 71

THE BEE STING

May 30, 2020, Day 71. Another lovely day. I'm going out this afternoon to my dear brother Bill and Sister-in law Bettylou McNamara's It's her birthday. So I gotta do it. I even baked cupcakes. Taa daa. I'll do 6ft. And now for the rest of the story. Way back in the early 60's. I had three baby in three years at 23. Then we got a TV.!! Kendra came 5 yrs later. I could not have done it with out Kenneth (he was a take charge, hands on Dad.) And Dr Bliss, pediatrician. She was so good and so blunt. But I respected this Dr. so I asked her once how long I have to boil the raw milk from the cows for the baby? She answered. Why are you boiling it is your husbands barn dirty? I said no, so she said then don't boil it. I told her once I thought the girls had the measles. Looking over her little glasses she asked me Where did you get your Degree. It WAS the measles. But she said nothing about my diagnosis. But one of the best reason I loved her is she saved my Kim's life. Kim got stung by two yellow Jackets and started itching profusely. We were eating dinner. So Ken picked her up and took her and put her in the tub. But then yelled out to me. Call the Dr., she is swelling up like a balloon. Dr Bliss came right on the phone and said get her right to the ER, I'll be waiting. When Ken pulled up she was waiting outside with needle in hand. Gave her a shot right there and then in the parking lot. They took her into the ER and the Dr stayed right there. The first shot did not work so another was given. She said if this does not work Mr. Huber we will have to do a tracheotomy. Well that shot worked. Thank God and Thank Dr Bliss. Kim had to have a series of immunization shots and we would go to her office 3 times a week $2.00 each nurse visit. When the Dr realized this was happening she said your husband has given shots to the cows hasn't he? I said yes, so she asked then why are you coming in here spending your money?

She gave me needles and serum for Ken. (can you imagine???) Poor guy, He hated giving them it as much as Kim hated them. This was another part of the good ole days. If we had had to check in, find a Dr to assess the situation, tell our insurance and give all our information I doubt if the outcome would have been the same. We were so lucky to have such competent, caring Dr people with out the kind of patient load our poor providers have now. The end. Be safe stay the 6 ft and wear your mask. Kiss the babies.

Day 73

THAT'S REALLY NICE

June 1, 2020, Day 73. Good morning. Great day. Just a little chilly to be out in the deck. Hoping Soon we will be together.. And now for the rest of the story. I worked at CHP Community Health Plan For 14 years. It was without a doubt the best group of people in one place, ever. We sometimes had way to much fun. There were Four desks out front. I sat in one. Check in! And there were jokes. In today's world we would almost all been fired for sexual harassment. This particular story was going round in the building. There were three southern ladies sitting on a porch in South Carolina. With a real southern accent this needs to be told. Number 1 lady said. My Husband gave me a new Mercedes for Christmas. Number 2 lady said that's wonderful. And one third lady said. Thats reaally niiice Then number 2 lady said I got a new diamond ring 2 carrots. And the third lady said again That's really niiiice. Number 1 asked her What did your husband give you for Christmas. And number 3 answered Weill my husband, he sent me to Charm School. They both exclaimed why would he send you to charm school. She answered well I used to say. I don't give a flying F— k. and now I say that's really niiice! We had fun with that. And one morning one of our patients came in early. And was going on and on and on about just everything. A real braggart. Really full of herself. Well one of the front desk girls slipped away and used a phone in the back and called my phone. When I answered she said (that's really nice.) The woman was still in front of me. And I had to excuse myself, walk away really fast. The end. Stay safe. Wear your mask. Kiss your babies.

Day 76

THE NUNS

June 4, 2020, Day 76. Beautiful day. So sorry for the sad day of mourning and pain for our country. I haven't watched a lot of news lately. I'm a real ostrich when it comes to almost anything unpleasant! And now for the rest of the story. I think it's a big part of me that does not deal with trauma or drama, that's why I keep going back to happy days, easy days , good days. I can remember and doubt me if you must going down side stairs in the third Street level of St Mary's school @ age 4/5 My mother leaving me in kindergarten was not pretty. The next thing I remember we were all lining up and getting our shots. I'm not sure which shot, just watching others ahead of me getting theirs. Again not pretty. We tend to remember traumatic or very happy times. I'm sorry to say St Mary's was not my happy times. In 2nd grade I had braids. They were there for pulling I found out. I was and still am a talker which was not a good thing in parochial school. So this happened a lot. But I never told my mother. I may have told Jack. Then On to 3rd grade. And the Palmer method of handwriting. The paper had 3 lines and the object was to keep our circles or lines within the three lines. Without picking up your pencil!! Guess who had a problem not picking up their pencil??? Each time I would get hit from behind (never saw it coming.) with the biggest ruler I ever saw right on my knuckles. Was it only me??? They seemed to lay in waiting for me. Again not Happy. Add this feeling to thinking I was for sure going to Hell for my evil feelings about the Nuns. Then God heard me or my big brother Jack. He asked Mom if we could please go to Greenport School, just at the end of our street. (She never said the no word to Jackie) It also would have been so much easier and cheaper and I prayed she would see how much better. She said Yes and I went to 4th grade at Greenport. They put me back to Third after a few weeks. I was too young and too immature. When the third grade teacher said your lettering is very nice Elizabeth. I almost cried. I Thank you God Thank you Jack.

Day 81

POOR GUY ON THE PATH

June 9, 2020, Day 81. I actually worked today.
Went to Hyde Park to help with files. Hot day. I
threw off my clothes. Put on shorts and my favorite
Minnie Mouse TShirt. I'm sitting on the deck, fan
blowing on me. And now for the rest of the story.
I'm going to call this the poor guy on the path. This
is totally PG rated. So stop if you think you'll be
offended in any way. Way back In The High school
days I had an appointment over Street. (that's
Country talk) Dr. Dentist?? Not sure, not really
relevant. There is a path from Oakdale to the back
of the High school that pretty much we all took.
Down a hill and up a steeper one and you're there!
Well this day I was taking the path and I was
walking down the Hill yes walking. I noticed
someone up in the middle of the bigger hill. I was
a little nervous. But as I approached him he turned

around and had his private parts in plain view. Well I never ran so fast ever, anytime. As I passed him. I was screaming and never looked back again. At the top of the hill I began breathing again. I was screaming, and ran into the school to the office. The nurse took me under her wing. They called the Police and I told them exactly what happened. Thank the Lord they never found him. As time went by I had time to rationalize the whole situation. And I'll leave you with this. That poor guy was probably just going to the bathroom. I scared the Bejesus out of him. He most likely to this day is still having trouble going. My bad. Really bad. The end. Stay safe. Go out to dinner. Wear your mask. Kiss the babies.

Day 83

GOOD WAITRESS

June 11, 2020, Day 83. Rain this morning. Such a beautiful sound. Remembering the tin roof on our house at Maple Ave. My safe haven Listening to the rain on that roof. I am sitting out on the deck now. At peace. And now for the rest of the story. Way back in the day when my girls were little I waitressed at night so I could be with them during the day. I loved waitressing. I have an undying need to be the best I can at whatever job I have. So suffice it to say. I think I was a good waitress. I had someone say to me once. "Waitresses are a dime a dozen." I took offense and said. "But good ones aren't". One of my favorite places was Clover Reach in Omi. Billy Cranna was my immediate boss in charge of the kitchen. I would blow up FB if I went on and on about Bill. One night one of our members walked in, an attorney from Hudson. His wife went to another table to talk to someone. His three kids ran outside, he went to a big table of 8 and sat down. I went right over and asked if I could get him a cocktail. He ordered, said yes I want two extra dry Martinis straight up with a twist. I went to the bar, ordered, brought them back and meanwhile his wife joined him I placed one drink in front of her and one in front of him. (My bad assuming) He said really loud. Excuse me, What did I order??? I said two extra dry martinis straight up with a twist. He then really loud said thats what I ordered. She did not order. Because by the time it took you got back to me I'd be looking all over for you. And said to his wife under his breath (you can't fix stupid). I walked away and asked the other server "can you please take them? " she said sure, I heard the whole thing! I thought it was all over. But at the end of the night Bill said can I ask you what happened out there tonight??? I told him the whole story thinking he was going to be not happy with me. Bill said don't you ever allow that to happen to you again. You come get me, I'll handle them. I loved this guy so.. I have so many stories about my waitress career, I'll continue tomorrow. Enjoy the rain. Be safe. Wear your mask. Get your butts back to work. Kiss those babies and your cook.

Day 84

HOLE IN THE SCREEN DOOR

June 12, 2020, Day 84. Tea daa I was really actually out for appetizers and wine today, I worked til 4:30 and texted my baby sister. Do you want to meet for a drink. And she said the Yes Word. It was sooo nice by the waters being waited on. Water, boats, people and wine and my sister's company. Life is good. And now for the rest of the story. Way back when my Ken was with me when I was still working, my daughter Karen and husband Ricky had a yellow lab named Jack. She came to see her father because Jack had a hot spot on his hip. Ken treated it for her. But and that's a big but never mentioned it to me. Fast forward a week or two and my favorite person, my brother Jack ,came to visit. Had a wonderful time with him. He went home. Ken and I were sitting on the deck. Ken reading (absorbing) the Register Star. I was sitting next to him and asked him how the screen door got a hole in it.

Never looking away from paper he said When Jack was chasing Mollie (our Dog). I'm thinking about this. And asked Jack was chasing Mollie??? Now don't get me wrong my brother really loved our dog, but I never saw him chase her. I asked "Jack was chasing Mollie"??? And again , annoyed because I was interrupting his paper time, never putting the paper down He said, don't you remember Jack chasing Mollie and trying to smell her butt. I could not stop laughing. He was talking about Karen's dog I was talking about my brother Jack. Well. We had a lot of fun with that. Truthfully my brother Jack was never involved in that whole story. Be safe wear your Mask Stay 6ft. Kiss your babies.

Day 85

THE VIP PATIENT

June 13, 2020, Day 85. Cool day. Not on deck until 11:00. Quiet day. Book time. And I watched the West Point graduation Ceremony. Very moving. My favorite kind of No drama or fake news day. And now here we go. Way back in the CHP days I'm guessing. 90's. I was the check in and Dr receptionist. There was a head nurse, Lisa, that was such a nice person. Great at her job and such a calming effect. So consequently when anyone came through the front door bleeding. I would page Lisa. (Lisa to the front desk). She would laugh about this later in that she could always gauge the severity by the sound of my voice By octave's. She would appear like bewitched to save me (super Nurse). I did not do well with blood so she was great!!! One day there was an older man coming along the window out front and one of the girls at the front desks said OMG! he just went down. I paged Lisa of course and a few nurses came running and went right outside. Turns out they scared the hell out of him as he just was bending over tying his shoe. Another story. A lady came to my window and I said can I help you? She said I'm here to see Dr.X I believed at the time (don't quite know why) it was the Dr's mother. So I said I'll be right with you. I went around and escorted her back to the Dr.s office. I asked her if I could get her anything. And she said water. I got her a water made sure she was comfortable, And went back to my desk. A little later Dr.'s nurse (my Joy, loved this nurse) asked who is in Dr's office. I said his mother. She said. Who???? That's not his mother! Well it turns out it was his 11:00 appointment. Not his mother. I got so many laughs about that. But I believe in patient/customer service. I believe she told everyone about her health insurance. Like no other out there anywhere!!! That job was like no other. Find a job you love and you'll never work a day in your life, Is about that job. Still stay safe please. Mask's. 6ft. Kiss the babies and the cook.

Day 87

BRAVERY

June 15, 2020, Day 87. Another beautiful day out here on the deck, on the house that Ken built. Sitting and remembering. My favorite old lady pastime.. And now going back to Betty McNamara days. (before Tillson). This petite redhead (loved by so many) had a look that actually could turn you to stone. Fortunately only my brothers and I saw it. I need to lead in to this story. I did not like to be dared. Someone inside me said. Oh yeah watch this (a lot like hold my beer). At the end of Maple Ave was a down hill and a steeper up hill. Or reverse them if your coming back . Well we all had the skates that clamp on our shoes. I was always the last one out of the house as I could never find my key (that tightens these skates on our shoes.) Well my friends said I could not skate down the steep hill. Betty can tell me I can't. You all can't tell me!!!

And I said oh yeah watch this. It was all going good, and fast, and then faster and faster till I lost my balance. And finished halfway down the hill on my hands and knees. There are a lot of cinders on that hill and I believe 1/2 of them were imbedded in my knees. I guess I showed them. And fast forward to Our Stottville home. There was a huge water tower near our yard. I'm guessing 100 ft high. All I did was mention I would love to climb that, and again You can't reared it's head. Well I climbed the many steps to the top and sat up there. The view was spectacular. Busy looking out over the town. I never saw that little redhead pull in the driveway. I heard her yelling you need to come down here right now. Oh Lord. I saw the look from way up there. I came down. A hell of a lot slower than I went up. I was more afraid of her than the climb. She asked me what the hell I was thinking. Well turns out I did my thinking in my room for awhile. A few years later at Kelly's Bar my friends and I were sitting at a table, Ken Huber was sitting at the bar. Some one of the girls said do you know who would be a good catch ? (can you imagine). Kenny Huber. I looked him over from where I was sitting and said I think I'm gonna go talk to him. You wouldn't dare!! End of story. Actually the beginning. Be safe. Be careful. Wear your mask. Kiss the babies.

Day 88

FOOD FOR THE CHICKENS

June 16, 2020, Day 88. Another breathtaking glad to be alive day. Breeze. Not too hot. My Kasey came and mowed my lawn. If anyone needs their lawn mowed he is reasonable and does a really nice job. We are now out and about. But being careful. Think I'm going back to my waitress days. Clover Reach and the shenanigans. We had a huge child's sports banquet. seating was very crowed. Children, Parents. Grandparents, And the tables were long and close. We were serving dessert, my Butchie and I. She held the tray high, I grabbed the vanilla ice cream with Chocolate syrup and placed in front of each person. The aisle was just wide enough for us sideways. I went to place an ice cream dish in front of a child and he stood up abruptly as I as going over him, and his head butted my dish. The ice cream and syrup all went flying in the air onto a Nana's really pretty mint green pant suit. It was almost in slow motion, and it was a sight to behold. We all tried to make it better but we only made it look worse. We spread the chocolate around. Fast forward to another banquet. Same conditions. And my friend Butchie has the tray again. But with pie this time. I was serving. She thought she was at the end of the row and brought the tray down but there was a little old man under it and she hit him hard. We apologized profusely but he really was not sure what happened. Not sure if a concussion? We ran in the kitchen and were laughing like he— and Bill Cranna said. Now what did you two do? One night there was a gala event. Everyone was dressed to the nines. Long dresses. Very fancy. I was In My waitress attire. My mother in law was cooking and I was getting ready to go home and she said. Here take the garbage for the chickens (we had Chickens). It was a really big clear bag full and I tried to sneak out the side entry dragging my garbage. It's hard to be nonchalant when everybody is in gowns and your hauling garbage.

Well you've heard of Murphys Law. Well this is Bonnie's Law. Half way out the hallway the damn bag broke open. And there was garbage all over the hall. As we were cleaning it up there were so many more (oh you poor girl Looks). I wanted to just disappear. It's really not hard for me to be humble when life throws me these fun times. I still loved waitressing. Gotta take the good with the bad. And gotta laugh like hell. Be safe. Wear your mask. Kiss your babies go out to eat. Help our local restaurants.

Day 90

GEORGE

June 18, 2020, Day 90. Such beautiful weather. Sitting out now. Worked in HydePark today, nice quiet ride down. And now. Going back to Greenport school. 8th grade. We took field trips with two other schools. Stottville and Claverack. all before consolidating schools. We all graduated from our local schools and went on to Hudson High. All three schools were visiting Hyde Park and we were to take notes on Franklin Roosevelt's life and home. Well at 13. I fell in love with a Stottville boy named Danny. I was busy taking notes on him and where he lived. He was just the cutest boy in the universe. At the time I was still living at Maple Ave. I had Dan's sister fix it so we would meet at the old Community Theatre. Well I was in heaven. Dan had hitch hiked in with his friend George. But Dan sat with me. I guess maybe

George was jealous of his friend. I can still remember I had on a white blouse, starched collar and all, and thought I was the cats meow (an old phrase from the 50's). Well I'm sitting there feeling so good and something slaps me along side of the face, wet and running down my neck into my starched white blouse. A boy named George informed us he had been spitting In his hand for an hour. Snuck up behind me and he hit me with that. That is how I met George (not a fan of his) When i moved to Stottville, Freshman year, everyone knew the legend of George. He was always In trouble. And his Mom always covered for him and was his alibi all the time for everything. Our favorite saying was my Georgie would not do that. If you were in Kelly's and mentioned your car battery was crap. He would disappear. And later low and behold you had a new battery in your car He would have borrowed one for you from some poor person at the CMH or the Match factory working nights! But he was good to his friends. He was always in work dress and greasy fingers from borrowing batteries!-and working on cars. One night he asked my friend for a date. And she replied George when I need a grease job I'll go to the garage. He went out and pulled wires out of her car. (Our Georgie would never do that.) At Kelly's one night Ken mentioned he was looking for a boat, To no one in particular. The next morning on our lawn was a boat with NYS Dept of Conservation all over the side. Ken hunted him down and told him to come get that GD boat out of our yard. (our Georgie would not do that.) Moving on and up. George borrowed a motor from someone or someplace and was being chased by the police. He went across the Rip Van Winkle.Bridge, stopped on the bridge and threw it over the side, but!!!! the ice was frozen and it stayed on top of the ice. Well His Mom could not say not her Georgie. We had many laughs about George and his shenanigans. He was our Bonnie and Clyde all rolled into one. I don't mean to speak ill of those gone on but he was our Stottville legend. Moral, Moms. If they did it let them pay the piper. Fun times. Stay safe. Wear your mask. Love Your tribe.

Day 91

NO SOUP FOR YOU

June 19, 2020, Day 91. Another beautiful day. Hot but I'm on deck with fan on. I refuse to go in yet. Worked today. Now resting. Life is good. And now. Way back in the old days. 1963. Mrs. Huber (not me) got me a job at the Yorkshire Farms Motel cleaning motel rooms. I had my Kathy 19 months and Kimmy 3 months. It was July and August. And hotter than (well you know). I would clean 8-10 rooms in the heat. And the manager would always go ahead of me before I got there and take any tips left. I had a nice lady ask me if I had got her tip and then I knew. It was the worst job I ever had. The hottest summer I can remember and I was 22 yrs.old But we needed the $. (farmers Pay) So what does not kill you makes you stronger.. I still loved farm life To this day I always leave the hotel staff/help a nice tip. After that they wanted me to waitress at the Yorkshire Farms. I loved that Job. Paul Laporte was one of the best bosses ever. And there were still some obnoxious patrons. We had a retired judge that would come in always at closing time. And we would accommodate him. He had the sweetest wife that he would berate through the whole meal. (he brought her out of the slums, she was nothing till she met him, people felt sorry for him because she had no social skills (a really nice guy). Well on Saturday nights you could not move out there, the piano bar and so many Hudson people enjoying the music. This particular night I was in the kitchen and heard this judge yelling at my Boss; you have all your people padding our checks, you're charging us for things we never had your Robbing us all. So Paul came in the kitchen and said Bonnie did you charge so and so for Soup??? He said they never had soup. I looked at the check and said Paul that's not Soup it's Rouq, for rouquefort dressing on their salad. Soup is not .50 He lit all up and kissed my cheek. I could hear him shouting from the roof top. Did you have rouquefort cheese on your salad??? It Made Paul's night. I Loved the Yorkshire. I loved waitressing, loved helping out my Ken and again loved farm life. Much more to come on the Yorkshire. Stay safe. Love your tribe. Kiss your loved ones.

Day 94

KEN, MORTIFIED

June 22, 2020, Day 94. It's a little warm today. Hit Lowe's, Chatham, Homequest, DD iced coffee, picked up car at Toyota. And finally late lunch (or early bird special) at Kozels with Kasey Allan and Kim. Saw our favorite server Terry. Excellent as usual, good food too, as usual. And now. I'm going back again to the Yorkshire Farms day's. 1965. I was 24. There are so many stories. But I'll tell the ones that stood out. I had just started as a server when a very nice looking, nicely dressed couple came in. There was only one other party in the Dining room. I took their drink order. And they were ready to order. The husband was reading the paper. The lovely wife said. I'll have a steak rare and if it's not rare you're all going to hear about it. I said I would let the chef know (chef was Paul the owner). The husband dropped the paper halfway and so quietly ordered a steak medium. I took the order and told Paul just what she said. I served the steaks and asked was there anything else. Wifie said stay here, cause if this is not rare you're going to have to eat it. She cut in and it was rare. She threw the knife and fork on the plate and said I said rare this is not rare. You need to make me a rare steak. Hubby never raised his head just started eating his steak. In the kitchen, Paul said a few words. Slapped a new steak on the grill on minute slapped it over and said here. I took it out and again she said wait. Cut in and yelled this GD meat is raw. Can't you cook a GD rare steak here, And stormed out. Hubby still eating asked me for another drink and asked me please be sure to put both steaks on the bill. And at that time he left me a $20 tip. She got to sit out in the car and he took his time and enjoyed his paper. I still loved the other hundreds of nice customer's that passed through. Ken would come out to meet me Saturday nights at closing time and we would go out somewhere and have a drink together. This one really busy Saturday we were leaving and Paul said we need to have a drink on him. Well there was a really nice looking young man in the crowded bar and Ken said to me look at that SOB he keeps staring at you. Even with me with you. I have to admit I was a little flattered. I was an old married woman with three babies. I thought it was kinda nice. So again Ken said. Omg I'm gonna say something, He's still looking you over That's why I don't like you working in a bar. I replied I don't work In the bar. So I said let's get out of here. So we set the mood for that night and went to another bar and ended our night at Theresa's greasy spoon, a diner by he Park in Hudson. Well guess who was there? Yup, good lookin guy, And again Ken was steamed because again. he was looking at me. Well Ken went to the bathroom and came out a hell of a lot faster then he went in and his face was beet red. He said let's go now, and threw $$ on the counter and out we went. Well it seems that good looking was not looking at me after all. He was looking at Ken. Followed him into to the bathroom. It was one of those subjects we did not bring up again. EVER. But I had all I could do to keep from hysterical laughter all the way home. The end. Stay safe. Go out. But watch your mate in a crowd. And hold back that laughter.

Day 96

MY MOM

June 24, 2020, Day 96. Such a nice night. Sitting out on the deck on the house that Ken built. But I'm going back to Maple Avenue and Betty Tillson. It's so true you never appreciate someone until they are no longer here. She was tough but a strange tough. I was a freshman in HHS and decided I did not want to go to school one day. So I went behind the house and sat on the porch. The dog came back there and Dewey followed. When Mom came out to get him in the car. He kept saying Bonnie.!! So mom came around the corner and I was snagged. The jig was up. Game over. And she laughed and said "you need a ride to school?" Not mad at all just took me to school. Another time my friend Linda and I planned to play hookey and I told Mom I did not feel good. Well Linda came to the house and Mom was running late so she said.

"Come in Linda, and you girls can watch Dewey and Denise if your not going to school today." Again not really mad. My curfew In High school was to be home before my mother and Mom liked to go out. So every friend in the school wanted to sleep at my house Jack had gone in the Navy. Bill in the Marines. Soooo Junior year I said Mom I want to quit school. She asked me why, was I going In the service?? And that was the end of that! Someone told her they saw me smoking and all she said. Bonnie if your going to smoke don't smoke on the street it looks terrible. From that day forward I never ever smoked on the street But I also saw the wrath of Betty. I had a cousin Marcy visiting. I was 12. She was moms Brother's daughter. There were three of us going to sleep out in a tent in the yard at moms friends house. The grownups were all in the house. While we were outside teasing Marcy, hiding on her and being mean, actually (Bullying) we thought it was funny. And about the third time Marcy went and told my mom (who obviously to me did not think it was funny) came out of the house, grabbed me by my ponytail and escorted me home through a shortcut. Took me In our house and said now go to bed you are not sleeping out. My headache from the escort home lasted a few days. Later on when she got really sick she was on oxygen and confined to the house for awhile. Never, ever, ever complained. I would go over do a few things for her and we had to have a cocktail. About 2 weeks before she passed we had our cocktail and I was leaving. She held her glass up to me, and I said you want another drink?? Laughing. She replied "well you can't fly with one wing Bonnie", I loved it. She was 94! Just never got to tell her how unique and special and loved she really was. When people say your just like your Mother. Not even close.

Day 100

LOSING A CAR

June 28, 2020, Day 100. Hello to all the graduates out there. And their proud Families. I'm so pleased you all get your day of all about you and your accomplishments, congratulations And, Now of course it's about me. Way back in the day 1957. My brother asked Mom if he could take us (Jack, Edie myself and Brad) to Coney Island. She could never say no to Jack (truth) so she agreed but told him to park about 250th street and take the subway in. Well we did just that and had a really good time. Except, my guy Brad at the time. He was the dearest, nicest guy you would ever get to meet. The only thing wrong with Brad was he was not Ken. Well Brad talked me into the Cyclone Roller Coaster. I guess I weighed 95 lbs. at the time. There was a wooden bar across our laps holding us in, And Brad was holding on to me to. Then we got to the top and went up and over the down hill. Well I came out of the seat and was about hip level over the track, fearing I was gonna come all the way out and die on the track. He was busy just staying in his seat. No regard for my demise. Which was seriously serious. With each hill we went over and down and over again I thought it was the end of me. But it was every man for himself. I was traumatized for sure. We got off the damn ride and I did not talk to him for awhile. He did not get it. It's supposed to be about me!!! Well we all had fun, stayed too long. Got too late and dark and we took the subway back. Well then we could not find the car. We got off on 250th Street. But no car. We all looked for about an hour. And decided it was stolen. Jack called Mom and said that someone stole our car. she laughed. And said are you 250 West or East. We had the right Number. Close but no cigar. We had to figure it out. We did finally go East and found the car and headed home. Betty always gave us plenty of rope to grow with. It worked. We are really none of us afraid to leap. As a mother I worried about everything that could happen always! She said don't worry til something happens then is time to worry. You worry about worrying. I try people but again I'm not Betty. She was a Special lady. Stay safe, kiss the babies.

Day 101

MY BIG BROTHER

Day 101   I'm at peace. The rain and thunder and lightning do that to me. I hope your all doing better now that the doors have opened up a little. Stay safe though. And this story is not about me (if you can believe that), it's about my big brother Jack. John Edward McNamara, III. He is a story in itself ,that guy. When Mom was a single mother she relied on him for almost everything. When she was working two jobs he was 11 and making us grilled cheese, tomato soup and 1/2 loaf of wonder bread. Tuna, hamburgs all kind of good meals. He at 12 was delivering milk before school in the AM. Being the man of the house for my mother and taking so much off her plate. When Mom remarried he was 16. and had trouble giving up the reins. He hitchhiked to an Air Force base in Columbus, Ohio to visit an uncle In the service that he admired a lot to find out all about the armed forces. My mother's sister called her to say he was there. Mom was quite relieved. He stayed on the base for a few days and they put him on a bus home. He said mom never said a word. Just picked him up in Albany. He always did well in school. Would read his books, put them in his locker and remembered what he had read. Next thing I know he just turned 17 and told my Dad that Mom said he could join the Navy if Dad would sign. (Mom had not said that). Dad said he thought it was a good idea and that was that. Mom did not sign. But he only needed 1 signature. Quit after his Junior year and left us. He did fly home from California to go with me and Brad and Edie to the Senior Prom. He did so well in the boot camp and testing that the Navy sent him to Cornell University. An Ivy League School. All with out a high school diploma. From there he became a Lieutenant Commander. Not to tacky for a Maple Avenue boy. He took such good care of Betty Tillson. (he saw how hard she worked.) He sent her to Switzerland, on Cruises, to

Las Vegas (Many times), Florida, Texas, Virginia, all over the place. She so loved being spoiled! Ken and I spent every vacation with him wherever he was stationed - they were the best of friends. They were the best of times. He even took us to the Masters! When Ken passed so did the baton. To him. He took over being my rock, my confidant, my financial advisor, My shoulder, my everything. This is just a big thank you, I so appreciate you. You take care of everyone. You are Smart You Are Kind You are Beautiful. One thing I know nothing compares to you. I did not have room to tell you about his lovely wife and children and grandchildren. Coming soon in a FB story near you.

Day 102

1963 DODGE MONOCO

Day 102 Good Morning. Just a beautiful day. Went to a 4th party yesterday. Ann and Guy's house. Great food, great band and really great company. We tried to maintain 6 ft.. And now some reflecting as I'm sitting on the deck. Ken always accused me of being heavy handed and I never quite knew how right he was until way back to the day. I took my girls to Sunday School every Sunday (I felt they should have the knowledge and then when older they could make intelligent choices) Well the minister asked if I would teach Sunday School. (Can you imagine that?) At this time we had an 8 year old Dodge Monaco. I feel 20 feet long big station wagon. It had no power steering and no power brakes. Just had the shifting lever on the column. This particular Sunday, I was leaving the church. Girls all in ready to go. Started her engine up and shifted into first. But, And this is what the story is about. The shifting lever came off in my hand. I knew this could not be good. I went to the ministers door and asked to use the phone. (No Cell Phones) the silent ages. And when Ken answered I said "Honey I'm in the ministers office" (to give him a heads up no yelling or swearing) when I divulged the reason I was calling. My rock came right away, shook his head, put the car in one of the gears and told me to drive it home. When at home. He said. JC Bon, I know 200 pound men that could not shear off a shifting lever!! Somehow I felt that was not a compliment!!! So that is when I actually realized he was right, I am heavy handed!! Our new car had power steering.!! Win win. Stay safe wear your masks. Kiss your cook.

Day 103

ICE PRINCESS

July 1, 2020, Day 103. What I feel good day. Lovin the rain. Lovin the quiet. And now it's the Maple Avenue Princess of the Ice. No it was not me, not the princess type. Way back in the day Late 50's I think, the Niagara Mohawk electric company on Fairview Ave. had a small body of water behind it with access to it from Maple Ave. I believe there were 10-15 kids would ice skate there. This particular day someone decided we needed a princess of the pond and all took a vote. Well my little blonde blue eyed friend Elaine got the most votes. And when iI figured out how many, one of my brothers even voted for her. I just never knew which one. My mom worked so hard to give us what we needed and also what we asked for. I had begged for ice skates and Betty found the money and bought them. I was on cloud nine the, fluffiest one ever. Well that winter, I was only not the chosen princess, I fell through the ice with one foot. Then I found out the ice was not over water, it was over tar. One of my brand new sparkling white Christmas skates was covered with tar. We did not have Dawn back then. so I could not get it clean. I could not tell my mom, she spent so much on those skates. So I never mentioned it. I would go and skate with my lovely red rubber boots. (princesses do not wear red rubber boots). She never knew.. We would swim at Bunkers bridge, Further up behind where Healys let his cows pasture. I loved cows even way back then. The water was very muddy and murky on the bottom. We found that out when my brother's friend grabbed my bike and rode it off the bank into the water, never to be seen again. They could not find it. Betty was not happy! We had such freedom on those summer days. 9:00-6:00 we were on our own. It was the best of times definitely not the worst of times. Best childhood ever!! And not a lot of monetary value. I need to lighten this up a bit.

There was a radio station at the end of the street WHUC. I decided at 11 or 12 I wanted to sing on the radio. (shy child). I asked my friend. to go with me. She would not sing. So I sang alone. My debut was Mocking Bird Hill! I believed I was spectacularly good. Some people even told me they heard me. Did not need to be a princess I was a Star. Stay safe out there. Kiss the babies. And your significant other.

Day 105

PHASE III

July 3, 2020, Day 105. My last COVID-19 post. Columbia County did well!! We're all free to roam about the NYS Taa daa. We are allowed in restaurants. I went to Creekside Restaurant for my sister Denise's Birthday. It was so nice to be out with loved ones, laughing, talking, masking. Maintaining 6 feet. We sure appreciate things when they're missing from our lives. It's like deferred gratification. So happy when it finally happens. I think we will not be taking a lot for granted from now on. I can't wait to see you out and about. I will want to hug you. But I know not yet. not quite yet. Just to see my friends will suffice for now. My condolences to all who did not make it out. To all the survivors of this horrid virus, Cause for celebration. We are NY strong. Still stay safe, wear your mask, do 6 ft. And kiss the babies. And your significant others and please follow the One way arrows in Hannaford. It's not that difficult People

About the Author

Elizabeth McNamara Huber, (Bonnie) lives, in Ghent, New York, a small town near Hudson, in the Catskill Mountains. She is the mother of four, grandmother of five, and a great-grandmother of six At 79, she still works for Conifer Realty as a consultant for their many sites in the Hudson Valley.

Caught in the New York State COVID-19 lockdown in March, Bonnie found the political fights and anger on FACEBOOK to be offensive, and felt the need to share a lighter side of life by posting her daily activity, along with countless reflections from her life growing up in rural America in the past 70 years.